For everyone who has trouble speaking, trouble being heard,
for everyone who has lived without understanding on their side –K.K.Y.

For my parents –J.L.

Text copyright © 2024 by Kao Kalia Yang
Illustrations copyright © 2024 by Jiemei Lin

Carolrhoda Books®
An imprint of Lerner Publishing Group, Inc.
241 First Avenue North
Minneapolis, MN 55401 USA

For reading levels and more information, look up this title at www.lernerbooks.com.

Designed by Emily Harris.
Main body text set in Horley Old Style MT Std.
Typeface provided by Monotype Typography.
The illustrations in this book were created with digital painting technology.

**Library of Congress Cataloging-in-Publication Data**

Names: Yang, Kao Kalia, 1980– author. | Lin, Jiemei, 1989– illustrator.
Title: The rock in my throat / Kao Kalia Yang ; illustrated by Jiemei Lin.
Description: Minneapolis : Carolrhoda Books, [2024] | Audience: Ages 5–10 | Audience: Grades 2–3 | Summary: "In this moving true story, Kao Kalia Yang shares her experiences as a Hmong refugee child navigating life at home and school in America while carrying the weight of her selective mutism" —Provided by publisher.
Identifiers: LCCN 2023021858 (print) | LCCN 2023021859 (ebook) | ISBN 9781728445687 (lib. bdg.) | ISBN 9798765611876 (epub)
Subjects: LCSH: Yang, Kao Kalia, 1980-—Juvenile literature. | Hmong Americans—Biography—Juvenile literature. | Selective mutism—United States—Juvenile literature. | Immigrants—United States—Biography—Juvenile literature. | Refugees—Thailand—Biography—Juvenile literature. | BISAC: JUVENILE NONFICTION / Social Topics / Depression & Mental Illness
Classification: LCC E184.H55 Y37 2024 (print) | LCC E184.H55 (ebook) | DDC 973/.0495972092 [B]—dc23/eng/20230523

LC record available at https://lccn.loc.gov/2023021858
LC ebook record available at https://lccn.loc.gov/2023021859

Manufactured in the United States of America
1-50265-49877-8/9/2023

# The Rock in My Throat

written by **Kao Kalia Yang**

illustrated by **Jiemei Lin**

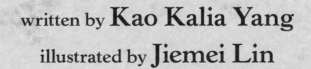

Carolrhoda Books

Minneapolis

Recess is the hardest time of the day.

All the kids are playing. Some are on the playground, and others are in the field by the side of the school. There's a group on the pavement in front of me.

The teachers are all busy watching over the kids and talking.

I look at the sky.
I look at the ground.
I look at my feet.
I look at my hands.
I look all around so the people can't see
that I'm lonely.

I am relieved when I see a feather
on the ground. It is a gray feather,
a small one, like dandelion fluff
only a little bigger.

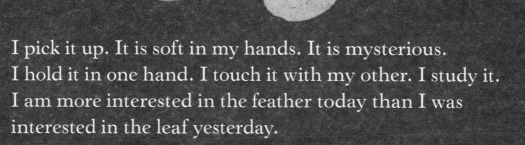

I pick it up. It is soft in my hands. It is mysterious.
I hold it in one hand. I touch it with my other. I study it.
I am more interested in the feather today than I was
interested in the leaf yesterday.

After school, I tell my mother about the sky and the ground. I tell her my feet are small, but my hands might grow large. I tell her about the feather I found, the feather I have in my pocket.

My mother says in Hmong, "Kuv tsis paub ua cas koj tsis hais lus tom tsev kawm ntawv."

Her words make me stop talking. I feel the feather in the pocket of my jeans become smaller and smaller. Inside my pocket, my right hand reaches for the place where the feather is, afraid that it will disappear.

Later, I look at my mother across the table from me.

I will never tell her about the moment I decided to stop talking if I can help it. I don't want to be like the many people who speak English. There is a rock in my throat now, and it grows heavier by the day.

I don't want to be like the woman in the store. The woman who tapped her hand on the counter when my mother tried to ask where the light bulbs were but didn't know the English words. The one who looked away when my mother said, "I'm looking for the thing that makes the world shiny."

The English words in my mother's mouth were sweet and sticky like candy, and they wrapped themselves up in her teeth. Her tongue tried to free the words, but it took time. Time that the English-speaking people don't have.

That day, the woman grew bigger
and bigger behind the counter.

My mother and I grew smaller and
smaller in front of it.

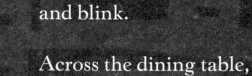

Now, I blink and blink
and blink.

Across the dining table,
I shrug at my mother,
letting my shoulders go up
and then down.

I say, "Kuv tsis paub thiab."

At first, no one noticed when I stopped talking at school.

I continued to sit at my assigned desk.
I continued to keep my desk clean, my hands to myself.
I continued to keep my eyes on the teacher at the front of the classroom.

One day, our teacher is sick. We have a substitute who looks a lot like our teacher. She doesn't know who any of us are, but she has a list with our names on it. She calls them one by one. My last name starts with a *Y*, and I know I'm last.

I try to clear my throat. I listen as all the kids say, "Here" when their names are called. Trying to get the air out of my mouth feels like I'm pushing my heart up into my throat.

When the teacher says, "COW YAN," I really try to say "here," but the only sound I'm able to make is a shaking cough.

She says, "Louder," scanning the room, trying to find me among the desks.

The teacher finds me because all the other children are looking at me.

They are not all mean looks. A few of them, the nice ones, show on their faces that they hurt a little for me.

I dig into the carpet of our classroom with the tip of my shoes.

I want the floor to open up and suck me down, through the thin carpet, through the thick cement, through the pipes, through the basement, through the ground, all the way to the core of the earth, so that the burning in my face would feel cool next to the plasma underneath everything.

Instead, I raise my hand, feeling the heat rise from my throat.

The substitute looks at me and smiles. "Next time, speak a little louder."

All day long, the volume of my listening to her voice is turned up on high.

I can't focus on the math problems on my worksheet.

When it is freewriting time, I can't write anything at all.

Every time she asks a question, I look away so she doesn't ask me anything.

I am exhausted when I get home.
I am exhausted every day after that.
I am exhausted every time I go to school.
I am exhausted every time we are in the
world that speaks English.

The only place I am able to rest is at home. Everyone at home speaks Hmong: my mother, my father, my older sister, and my aunts and uncles and cousins when they visit. Everyone speaks normally to everyone else. It is a song, uninterrupted, and it flows and flows.

It is time for parent-teacher conferences.

The teacher sits on one side of the table.

My father, mother, older sister, and I sit on the other.

The teacher wants to know, "Does COW speak at home?"

My sister says in Hmong, "This teacher also wants to know if Kalia speaks at home."

My father and mother look at each other, and then my mother says, "Tell her Kalia speaks all the time."

My sister says in English, "My mother wants me to tell you that at home COW speaks all the time."

The teacher bites her bottom lip a little and flattens the line of her mouth, looking at me like I'm a puzzle.

The teacher stops biting her bottom lip, and the corners of her mouth lift in a smile.

She says, "COW is doing well in everything, but she won't talk at school."

I turn the volume of my listening down. I focus on the wall behind my teacher's head. I imagine the concrete crumbling and the world outside coming in. The birds. The wind. The leaves touching at their tips. They are clapping for me, but the hands in my lap are clasped tight together.

In the car, on the way home, my family is quiet. Once in a while, my father looks at me through the rearview mirror. My mother turns her head to check on me. My sister pats my hand. They all feel bad for me.

I feel bad for all of us.

Our brown car coughs into the air every few seconds.

Puffs of smoke rise behind us. No one says anything.
I know we all have rocks in our throats, and each of us
is trying our best. The problem is that mine has grown
too big and heavy for me to move.

Recess is the worst time of the day.

The pebble I've picked up is the size of the tip of my little finger. Its surface is gray, but it has speckles of white. In the light of the sun, on my palm, the white sparkles like diamonds. It is the most interesting thing I have ever seen in my life.

The girl in front of me speaks very clearly and slowly. She says, "Do you want to play with me?"

All of my heart wants to play with her, but the weight of the rock is too heavy for my tongue to lift. My throat works, but the words don't come out.

The rock grows bigger and bigger as the seconds pass. I don't know how to dislodge it, so I grip the little pebble in my palm. I don't look at her, and I shake my head no.

When she walks away, I repeat her name again and again, "Julia, Julia, Julia Chang." I tell myself, "One day, maybe she can be my friend."

## Author's Note

I was six years old when my family came to America as refugees of war from the camps in Thailand. For the first years of my life, Hmong was the language that I had built my home in. When I entered school, English was everywhere. Slowly, I picked it up in bits and pieces. I liked the way the words tasted different in my mouth, the way they did not need more air to float, the way they connected to one another, not like words holding hands but like magnets and metal. Everything changed when I was seven years old.

I became a selective mute in English halfway between first and second grade. I stopped talking at school. I got by with nodding and doing the thumbs-up. In fact, I wouldn't speak in English voluntarily until I went to college. In college, I learned how to whisper. When I became a writer, some of my childhood teachers came to my events to hear my voice. They knew me—they all said I hadn't changed much, but they had never heard me talk before. A few of them wept hearing my voice for the first time.

One of the big questions, in all my years of silence, was, Why?

At forty-three years old, I'm finally ready to answer. This book is that answer. I'm answering the children who asked the question directly and sincerely all those years ago when I couldn't answer them, the children who were trying to understand. I'm answering the children who, like me, were also quiet and weren't sure why or were afraid of hurting the people around them with their honest answers. I want each child who is afraid to talk, unable to find

Kalia on top of a dome-shaped structure at a playground in the McDonough Homes housing project, Saint Paul, Minnesota, 1988.

the words, to know that sometimes it takes a long time for us to understand, and an even longer time to express ourselves. I'm answering the question for the second-grade child who was me, young Kalia who wanted and wished desperately to one day be able to answer this question for herself, her teachers and, especially, her family.

Mother, you used to say, "Kuv tsis paub ua cas koj tsis hais lus tom tsev kawm ntawv." *I don't understand why you won't speak at school.*

I used to tell you, "Kuv tsis paub thiab." *I don't know either.*

Mother, I can tell you now. As a child, I saw the people who spoke fluent English walk away from your efforts to be understood and I felt your pain. I couldn't protect you, so I did the only thing I knew to do: I stopped talking in English. It was my great revolution against a world I knew was not listening to you. I couldn't control when the rock in my throat started weighing me down. I felt sad and sorry that I couldn't speak for myself or you for so many years. But those years have come and gone. I now know that sometimes the words that I cannot speak into the world, I can write in it.

Now, when I think back to all those silent years, when I listened and listened, I am filled with gratitude for all the lessons I learned. I'm thankful that I know to be patient when others are struggling into language. I understand so well what it is like to be lonely and, in the end, to love and appreciate the people who offer friendship.

Julia Chang became my friend, first through the letters we wrote to each other, and then later through the life experiences we shared.

**Hmong** is pronounced MOHNG. The word refers to a language as well as to a people, an ethnic minority, from Southeast Asia. Starting in 1975, many Hmong families came to the United States as refugees of war.

**Kao Kalia** is pronounced KOW kah-LEE-uh. It means *the girl with the dimples.*

**Kuv tsis paub thiab** is pronounced GOO CHEE POW TYA. It means *I don't know either.*

**Kuv tsis paub ua cas koj tsis hais lus tom tsev kawm ntawv** is pronounced GOO CHEE POW OO-a KYA KHAW CHEE HAI LOO THOH CHAY GUH DHUH. It means *I don't understand why you won't speak at school.*